How to disappear

Kendall A. Bell

Maverick Duck Press

© 2023

www.maverickduckpress.com

Second Edition

Cover art by Kendall A. Bell

ISBN-13: 979-8-88596-890-4

Contents

I am breaking my bones to fit into places

I desperately need to be, like the curve
of your legs, the arch of your foot. Like
the Golden Gate Bridge, the coastline of
Nova Scotia, the sleeves of your jacket.
I push my achy joints to their breaking
point to touch the things you've left
behind, like your headphones, the cord
balled up in knots, like the dog, who is
confused and missing you. I listen closely
for the snap. It is when I love you the most.
It is the only gift I can give you now that
you've put on your boots and took that swan
dive. I want to be that brave. I want us
to fuck boneless. I want redemption.

The distance between us

is the sound of voices streaming over
the internet, the long stretches of
flatlands. It is tolls and bridges
over rivers and industry. It is the
flashing cursor in notepad, the words
forming from fingers. It is the empty
wind of April, pushing you further from
me. It is the silhouette in the light
of morning, miles away in a kitchen.
It is the hole in me, never filled in
your absence.

The night we tried to run away

I didn't make it back in time to
pick you up from work. You gave
in to your nerves, hid in a fort
made of blankets. I made the mistake
of texting you the words "I love you."
You enrolled in culinary classes at
the local college. I spent the night
convincing myself that you would ditch
me for a late night Walmart run. You
couldn't bear to share the space between
your arms with me.

This world is only gonna break your heart

So I left you sitting at a table at some
truck stop diner off of a dusty interstate
in the middle of nowhere. The bill is paid,
the tip, still on the table. You won't find
my car in the parking lot, just the tire
marks left behind in the gravel and dirt.
There is nothing else I can give you besides
a full belly, an unwanted inconvenience.
Words will leave you as empty as that Coke
bottle rattling around the highway's edge.
I do this only to prove that I've never been
anyone's answer. I say these things to show
you that I am as broken as you, that you
cannot gather two shattered things from the
ground and make them one breathing thing,
something that won't end up as roadkill,
fed on by crows and flies.

What to do when your friends become ghosts

Hollow out the pages that hold their names -
names like Natalie and Alexa, names like
Bristol and Rachelle. Hold a wake with one
candle, one blood red rose. Have long talks
in the bathroom into the shower, listen for
the echo and swear it's someone who cares.
Fall asleep with the tv on and pretend its
a lullaby. Ball up your comforter and wrap
your legs around it like the morning after
a long night of drowning in tears and the
sweat of sympathy sex. Put on your mask and
walk into the pink and purple sky of an April
morning, carry your heart to the curb for
trash day.

Erasure

Your body is limp, like a child
using dead weight, passive
resistance. Your limbs are flesh
colored anchors splayed on floor,
pointing towards purgatory.
There is a pulse.
Refusal is in the permanent ink
of your script. My words crash
against the wall and shatter,
those disregarded, invisible sounds.
I cannot pull you from your sleep
ambivalence anymore. You breathe
and eat, sqwauk and stumble.
Nothing more.
Here is your perfect bound story
in fine print. The pages with my name
are in erasure.

Were you dazzled by the same constellation?

The one that shines brighter than any
night sky that draped over our old,
outdated house? You raise a finger
and play connect the dots with the
stars, each shining like holes in the
black paper of a Lite Brite. We look
for Venus, wonder if other galaxies can
see into our front yard, if they stare
at the overgrown evergreens and judge
us. I slip my goosebumped arm around
your back, your head still craned to
the sky. You are caught in some other
orbit.

South on the highway

It is not a crisis to want more than simple
niceties, to crave the passion that another
can give, through words on a screen, through
the softness in her dialect. We all want the
embrace in the doorway, the sound skin
makes when it brushes with another. We write
everything we dare not do - how the sweat
beading above her lip in the hot air feels
like salvation. How her legs glisten upon first
gaze - bare and smooth in the warm breeze.
How the tangle of limbs can be a kind of
nirvana, a rescue, a redemption.

We'll soon see if you'll be my ruin

As the ants crawl from cabinet to stove,
as the wasps nest in between the front
door and the storm door and chase me
from any chance of escape.
As the walls thin from being eaten from
the inside and the broken faucets leak
droplets of lives - lives that sit dormant,
break away from talk and touch.
As you turn away from my lips.
As you release into the pungent air of this
blackened room - unresponsive and unrepentant.

Open season

It is a Pandora's box of forevers
left out on the unmade bed, the sun
curling up the edges of yellowing
pages of promises unkept. It is the
curtains removed from windows, wide
open for peering eyes - a gateway
for ghosts of the past to reclaim
what they never relinquished. It is
the back door, pinned against the
dented and bruised dry wall, a path
to discovery, to limbs in frozen
animation, to the voices snuffed.
Do not mourn what cannot be missed.

I could be a ghost in your eardrum

Some piece of the past you've hidden
in a metal box that once held candy
or trendy underwear. I could be what
you've been embarrassed to admit to -
a mistake you can't erase, chalk on
your driveway that won't wash away.
I could be years of anticipation
that ended in disappointment when
the movie didn't deliver. I could
be worn sneakers in your trash can,
the insides splitting and peeling
up. Or - I could be the left corner
puzzle piece, just inside the border,
snugly inside the frame of you.

You hide and send out crumpled apologies

little pieces of paper with crossed out
words like forgive me, I screwed up
and I was hurt. The meaning is lost when
they end up as deleted drafts in your email,
torn Post-it notes piling in the mesh trash
can next to your desk. My calls keep going
to your voice mail. Thirty seconds later,
a text pops up with your name on it -
This isn't going to work anymore -
a convenient excuse to fuck someone else,
as if this familiarity has become our
undoing, as if this skin could be peeled
to be replaced with newness, a softer feel
against your chafed boredom. I am razor
burn on your legs, a dragged blade on dry
skin. There is no landscape left to explore.

The lullaby on the tongue is a sprout

It cannot grow to full size,
but regenerates over and over.
The repetition is what sates
all of the crying and incessant
wailing. I will rewrite these
words each day, until they fit
in your ears perfectly. They
will slowly make you love me
even though you swing balled
hands at my soft body. One day,
this song will be a record on
your turntable, a book of your
favorite poems. You will hold it
close at night and wish I would
sing it to you, but I will be ash.

You were the wrong exit

I wore you like a bruise,
weirdly shaped and purpled
on the back of my hand.
There is no pleasure in that
kind of pain. The slightest
graze and I wince. Your face
is a map to a dead end road.
In a matter of days, you turned
yellow, remained only a nuisance,
a faded book page, unable to inflict.

Feel like giving up

It doesn't just sneak up on you.
It's handed to you in a flask
on a bus, in a paper bag, incognito.
If I could, I'd smack it out of your
hand before it had the chance to turn
you into the slurred version of you
that stumbled in the background with
the lights dimmed, your microphone
shut off. The feet that once lifted
you would betray you, but there was
still your baritone, the pain echoed
how your body was beating you to a
pulp, how you dulled it in the bottles
hidden around your house, in your car.
You sank money into a failed venture
with a mistress, bred uncontrollably
but never found contentment. You found
an alley, and the second shot put it
forever out of reach.

For the girl who ran away

The book and two movies you lent me are
sitting on the bookshelf in my office.
I'm not done with them yet, though
you might be done with me. It has been
nearly three weeks since I saw your
face, thirteen days since you posted
a writing prompt on your blog. You
became a weekend migraine's victim,
a flowered dress on Easter. You are
a phantom behind a screen, a poet with
no words to offer. The curtains are
gathering dust. Soon, they will crumble.

Amanda spends Saturday with indecision

The baby fusses in his crib, has no idea
that you are conflicted, that each day
is one that you circled on a calendar that
curls at the edges in the back of a closet -
a closet where boxes hold carefully chosen
clothes and stashed twenty dollar bills.
Your oldest wants something to eat. You
wonder if you will have a yard big enough
to hold all of his toys, if they will fit inside
of a U-Haul. It is a constant back and forth,
a note on the kitchen counter, an unspoken
goodbye left for someone bereft of emotion.
Your sadness spreads like sickness, leaves
you seeking another skin to inhabit, another
body to deal with the rebuild. There is
nothing easy about losing years, about pages
torn in a book you thought was a fairytale.
Your aching back keeps your mind distracted
until you are left alone again, until the
silence becomes too much to bear.

It was my reflection I was avoiding

the marred surfaces of face and stomach,
the blue branches of blood pushed to the
surface among the blanched terrain. The
ache is invisible, is the quiet torture
that cannot be reflected in mirrors. It
was the impression of decline and defeat,
the spiral staircase of eroding promise
that might never had been borne of this
body to begin with. I sit in rooms unable
to cast shadows. I have shattered every
light bulb in the middle of the street—
no speculum is safe between these walls.

Sometimes affection is a salve we rub over affliction
(after Sarah Matthes)

Something to cauterize a wound that keeps
opening with every misstep, with each of
our grievances. Sometimes, affection is
the lost dog that never returns home, is
never found, maybe living with a loving
family in a town a few miles away, unless
it is the victim of carelessness, rotting
on the shoulder of the road, just feet
away from a diner. We fall asleep with our
hands clasped, our heat a binding spell.
we always wake in separate rooms.

I am learning new ways to be empty

as bones crack, refuse to heal,
the marrow dried and lifeless.
The empty holds hope captive in
a basement with mold spores and
the corpses of centipedes—
a life that became a funereal
march, a pile of boxes that hold
the memories of want, of desire
unfulfilled. I forget the shape
of bodies, ghost touch the faces
of never lovers who escape spaces
like a last breath. I am bloated
with this expanse of nothingness.

When you are empty what fills you

but the timbre of voices that
linger in the ears like distant
birds that seek a warm sanctuary,
the low drag of a too short straw
in a too large cup, the intolerable
gravity that pulls at the knees,
that cups a hand over watery eyes
and whispers sleep, there is no one
coming to look for you. What fills
you is the brine of unwept tears,
the tenantless rooms that hold the
memory of promise, now a menagerie
of nonchalance.

My heart is closing like a fist

the deep thud now a murmur,
a slow moving pendulum in
the throes of death. My heart
is an empty palm, the creases
hardened and cracking, an
empty, weed infested parking
lot. It will wall itself off
from intimacy, isolate in a
coat closet through another
desolate winter. It is such
a useless organ, its beats
wasted and unrequited.

The middle ground of feeling everything and nothing at all

and ruin is waiting on the
sofa, its legs crossed and
impatient. Rest is a bandit,
is an escape artist i cannot
chain inside of an oak chest—
letdowns and breakdowns are
a twenty four hour marathon
without commercial breaks,
an elusive quietness separated
by an ocean, by a galaxy.
The lie is the band aid, the
masked emptiness left to fester
and harden in a pantry behind
expired cake mixes and a gallon
of water kept for an emergency,
never needed, like me.

Maybe I could come back to myself

and not want to slice pieces of me
down a slow draining sink. Maybe i
can learn how not to hate myself so
intensely, to find some kind of peace
in my own company—discover the softness
that has eroded into an overflow of
anger. Maybe the dread i wake with can
be shed like dead skin, left behind to
decompose like leaves gathered along a
rusted fence. Maybe there are arms that
will not release after a tentative hug—
an unquestioned and bottomless tenderness
in this turmoil that simmers endlessly.

How to disappear

Start deleting phone numbers backwards
to A, forget how to answer the phone.
Deactivate every social media account.
Save your voice only for singing in the
car, speak to no one at work, listen to
how many times your name comes up. (It
will be none.) Unscrew every CFL lightbulb
and donate them to Goodwill. Invest in
black curtains, for every room. Leave your
dog inside someone else's fenced in yard -
the one with big tires on the grass. Throw
your mailbox into the street. Wear a hoodie.
All the time. Never, never make eye contact.
Go for your walk, abandon your route, blend
into trees, into sidewalks and streetlights.

Kendall A. Bell's poetry has been most recently published in Hobo Camp Review and The Aurora Journal. He was nominated for Sundress Publications' Best of the Net collection seven times. He is the author of three full length collections, "The Roads Don't Love You" (2018), "the forced hush of quiet" (2019) and, "the shallows" (2022), and 33 chapbooks, the latest being "how does it end?". He is the publisher/editor of Maverick Duck Press and editor and founder of Chantarelle's Notebook. His chapbooks are available through Maverick Duck Press. He lives in Southern New Jersey.

www.ingramcontent.com/pod-product-compliance
Lightning Source LLC
Chambersburg PA
CBHW072144150726

48002CB00004B/1623